Simón Bolívar

South American Liberator

by Carol Greene

 CHILDRENS PRESS®
CHICAGO

This book is for Matthew Reat.

PICTURE ACKNOWLEDGMENTS
The Bettmann Archive—16, 22, 28, 40, 46, 52, 66 (top & bottom left),
67 (top), 68 (top), 70 (bottom), 71, 72, 88, 100
Historical Pictures Service, Chicago—Frontispiece, 8
North Wind Picture Archive—68 (bottom), 69 (2 photos)
© Chip and Rosa Maria de la Cueva Peterson—66 (bottom right),
67 (bottom left & right), 70 (top)
Cover illustration by Len W. Meents

LIBRARY OF CONGRESS
Library of Congress Cataloging-in-Publication Data
Greene, Carol.
    Simón Bolívar : South American liberator / by Carol
Greene.
        p.   cm.
    Includes index.
    Summary: A biography of the South American general
and revolutionary, often called the "George Washington of
South America," who helped liberate Bolivia, Colombia,
Ecuador, Peru, and Venezuela from the domination of
Spain.
    ISBN 0-516-03267-4
    1. Bolívar, Simón, 1783-1830—Juvenile literature.
2. South America—History—Wars of Independence, 1806-
1830—Juvenile literature. 3. Heads of state—South
America—Biography—Juvenile literature. [1. Bolívar,
Simón, 1873-1830. 2. South America—History—Wars of
Independence, 1806-1830. 3. Heads of State.] I. Title.
II. Title: Simón Bolívar. III. Series.
F2235.3.G8385   1989
980'.02'092—dc20
[B]
[92]   89-34663
                                                      CIP
                                                       AC

Table of Contents

Chapter 1

LITTLE PRINCE CHARMING

In 1783, the idea of revolution crackled like lightning around the world. The old ways of government are wrong, thought more and more people. Rulers have too much power. It is time for a change.

In North America, the lightning had already struck. The colonists had fought their revolution and in 1783, England recognized the United States as an independent nation.

France would have to wait another six years before revolutionaries would storm that dread prison, the Bastille, and knock the king from his throne. But the idea was there, flickering.

Even some South American countries, ruled by the iron hand of Spain, had seen sputterings of revolution. In 1781, desperate men in both New Granada and Peru stood up and demanded freedom. Spain quickly and cruelly silenced them, but their idea remained.

On July 24, 1783, a boy was born in a large, comfortable house in Caracas, Venezuela. His parents called him Simón José Antonio de la Santissima Trinidad de Bolívar y Palacios. Simón Bolívar was not an especially strong or healthy child. Just to look at him, one would never think that someday he would juggle the lightning bolts of revolution in five different countries.

But everyone who met him agreed that he was a charming child. His father, Juan, died when Simón was only three. That left his mother, María Concepción, his sisters, María Antonia and Juana, and his brother, Juan, to love and pamper him. They did a good job.

By the time Simón was six, his mother probably worried that he was getting a little spoiled. She hired a tutor to try to drum some knowledge into her young son's head. Miguel José Sanz was a respected man in Caracas. Everyone knew how brilliant he was. But even Sanz had his hands full with Simón.

"You are a horn full of gunpowder!" he told the boy one day when he had had enough.

"Then you'd better not come near me," replied Simón. "I might explode."

Actually, he learned easily—when he put his mind to it. But most of the time Simón's mind was somewhere else.

The Bolívars were a very rich family. Their ancestors came from the Basque village of Bolívar in northern Spain. But there had been Bolívars in Venezuela since 1548 and they had made money with silver mines, copper mines, cattle ranches, and plantations that grew sugar, cacao, and indigo. Simón's mother's family, the Palacios, owned a great deal of property, both in Caracas and in its nearby port of La Guaira.

Simón had all the good things money could buy and he knew how to enjoy them—especially horses. While he was very young, he had to ride a little burro, which nearly drove him crazy. Once he got into the saddle of a real horse, it was hard to get him out again.

His favorite place was San Mateo, the family's country estate in the Aragua valley about fifty miles from Caracas. Here stretched acre after acre of sugarcane, along with fruit orchards, a mill, and a rum distillery. A boy could ride all day and not run out of things to see and do. Of course it took over twelve hundred slaves to keep San Mateo going, but Simón did not see anything wrong with that. Slavery was simply part of the system in the world he knew.

In many ways he lived the life of a young prince and probably did not understand that he was not really free either. But the fact was that Simón and his family were Creoles. That meant that although their ancestors came from Spain, they had been born in South America.

The Spanish government was not about to let its Creoles in the colonies get too powerful. So it forced them to live under rigid rules and regulations. Creoles could not hold high offices in government, although they had to pay very high taxes. Spain told them what books they could publish and sell and what countries they could trade with (mostly Spain). Creoles could not get much education and only the richest could do much traveling.

Young Simón would not have noticed most of these rules as he trotted his horse through the streets of Caracas or galloped in the sun at San Mateo. He certainly would not have minded the rule about education if he had known about it. As far as he was concerned, education was a bore.

But when Simón was nine, his life began to change. First, his mother died. Then, a few months later, his older sisters married and moved away. That left only Simón and Juan Vicente—along with Hipólita, the black slave who had been Simón's nurse for as long as he could remember, and her helper, Matea.

Even a spoiled young prince has weak moments when he needs someone to hug him and tell him that everything will be all right. It was Hipólita who cared for Simón in these moments. He said later that she was the only real parent he had ever known. He never forgot her and made sure she received a pension when she grew old.

Meanwhile, Uncle Carlos had become his guardian and the parade of tutors went on. A priest, a monk, a German scientist, and a young poet all tried to wake up Simón's lazy mind. He did eventually learn to read and his favorite book was *Don Quixote* by the Spanish author Miguel de Cervantes.

Don Quixote is the story of an idealistic knight who dreamed great dreams and fought against evil wherever he found it. Simón loved the book and took it with him everywhere he went. He may even have dreamed some dreams of his own about becoming like the Don someday.

Then came his last tutor, a strange man called Simón Rodríguez. Rodríguez would not have met the standards set by any school system today. But he was exactly the right person for Simón Bolívar. When he first met his young student, Rodríguez himself was only about twenty. But he had already roamed all over Europe, reading and talking about philosophy—and running after women.

Now he found himself with a nine-year-old boy who barely knew how to write, but loved to read, who was small and not too strong, but could charm everyone in sight. Rodríguez firmly believed in the educational philosophy of the Frenchman, Jean-Jacques Rousseau, and decided to follow it with Simón. Rousseau taught that people were naturally good. It was civilization that ruined them. So if they wanted to become good again, they must go back to nature. And that is exactly what Rodríguez did.

He and Simón moved to San Mateo where they hiked, swam, and rode. The boy's mind must not be crammed with all sorts of useless information, said his tutor. Instead, he must learn to watch and listen to everything that went on around him. Then he must learn to act in response to what he had seen and heard.

Sometimes pupil and teacher would travel by mule to one of the Bolívar cattle ranches down in the hot, wet *llanos* (river plains) to the south. There Simón could race with the *llaneros* (cowboys) after wild horses, learn to tame them, and in general have a wonderful time.

For five years Simón received this unusual sort of education and he loved every moment of it. His body grew hard and strong and his mind became quick and lively. Simón Rodríguez had never had a better student.

Then another flash of revolutionary lightning lit up the South American sky, this time in Venezuela itself. It was only a small flash and, thanks to an informer, Spain quickly put it out. One of the chief revolutionaries escaped, but the other was caught and hanged. Then his head, arms, and legs were chopped off and displayed in iron cages on posts in various Venezuelan towns.

Worst of all, as far as Simón was concerned, was the fact that some people believed Rodríguez had been involved with the revolutionaries. Uncle Carlos and Simón's former tutor, Sanz, managed to get the teacher acquitted, but everyone agreed that he would be a lot safer if he left the country. So Rodríguez boarded a ship and sailed away to roam the world some more. Behind he left fourteen-year-old Simón, strong and alert now, but wondering what on earth he should do next.

Simón finally joined a little troop of soldiers his father had organized years before. He probably did not learn much from them, but he looked good in his uniform and enjoyed

14

parading around. He even became a lieutenant and suddenly women began to flirt with him. All that was fine, but it was not enough. Rodríguez had awakened his mind and now he felt restless, excited, and confused. Surely he should be doing more. But what?

At last his family came up with an answer. They had the money and the influence to send him to Spain and relatives there who would look after him. It was time he saw the land of his ancestors and learned what it had to teach him.

So in January of 1799, Simón set off for Spain. He was fifteen years old.

The Madrid Simón visited was an interesting and lively city.

Chapter 2

TRAVEL AND TRAGEDY

The ship's first stop was Veracruz on the Gulf of Mexico. This town was known as a breeding ground for yellow fever and Simón had no intention of staying there. Instead, armed with letters of introduction to assorted important people, he leaped onto a horse and rode off to Mexico City, some 260 miles away. Here he spent plenty of money and hobnobbed with the cream of high society, including the Spanish viceroy.

He soon learned that Mexico had had its share of tiny revolutions too, and that the Spanish government had stamped them out as quickly and fiercely as it had those back home. When the ship sailed on to Havana, Cuba, Simón made a point of talking with some Creoles there. It turned out that they were not happy with Spain's policies either.

Simón tucked all this new information away for future reference. He was not sure what else to do with it now. But someday he would know.

The ship took twenty-seven days to cross the ocean. Then, just after the sailors had sighted Spain, a storm bounced them up and down the coast for thirteen more days. At last, late in the spring, they docked and Simón set off for Madrid.

He found a colorful, bustling city of 200,000 people. He found palaces, churches, and grand homes at every turn. He also found intrigue. King Charles did not like being ruler. He was happier in his gardens than on his throne. His wife, Queen María Luisa, was a much stronger ruler. Unfortunately, she also carried on several secret love affairs—which everyone knew about. In fact, most of Europe pretended to be shocked to the core by the goings-on in the Spanish court.

Simón found out about all of this quickly, since one of the queen's lovers was a friend of the uncle with whom he was staying. One night Simón even had to help sneak María Luisa, who had disguised herself as a monk, back to her palace.

All in all, Simón did not approve. He did not think much of young Prince Ferdinand either when he met him. He and the prince were playing a game, something like racquetball, when Simón accidentally knocked off the prince's hat. Furious, Ferdinand stopped the game and ordered Simón to apologize. Simón would do no such thing. It had been an accident. Period. No one had been hurt and there was no need for an apology. Finally the queen, who had been watching, stepped in. She told her son not to be a fool and to get on with the game.

If this was what the royal house of Spain was like, thought Simón, he did not have much use for it.

Soon, though, his thoughts turned in a different direction.

He met a girl, María Teresa de Toro, and fell deeply in love with her. She felt the same way about him and so he asked her family for permission to marry her.

The de Toros liked Simón and thought he would make María Teresa a good husband. But he was still very young—just seventeen. So they told him to wait a year. Perhaps he could spend part of that time traveling around Europe. Simón's guardian in Madrid, the Marqués de Ustáriz, agreed with this verdict. He suggested that Simón work at his studies—especially French—for a while and then, early in 1801, sent him off to Paris.

France's own revolution had recently occurred and Paris still showed scars of the battles. But Simón barely noticed as he watched the French people hail their new first consul, a small, stern-looking man called Napoleon Bonaparte.

Now there was a hero, thought Simón. And he had done it all himself. Napoleon did not become first consul because he came from some rich or important family. He was head of France because of his own brave deeds and brilliant mind.

Before long, though, Simón began to wish that he were not in France at all. He wanted to be with María Teresa and the months seemed to crawl by as he wandered around in a sort of daze. Then, at last, the year was up and he dashed back to Spain. In May of 1802, he and María Teresa were wed in Madrid.

That same day they drove to Corunna and took a ship to

Venezuela. From now on, thought Simón, his life would be perfect. He and María Teresa would make their home at San Mateo, his favorite place in the world. There they would live comfortably and raise a family. From time to time, they might drive into Caracas to visit relatives and friends. He would be the happiest man ever born.

After a month of parties in their honor in Caracas, the young couple did settle down at San Mateo. Simón's former nurses, Hipólita and Matea, went with them and for a while, life was as perfect as Simón had thought it would be. Then María Teresa caught a tropical fever. Simón was frantic. He had his wife placed on a litter. Then he and some of his slaves set out to take her the fifty miles to Caracas where she could get better medical care. Along the mountain paths they hurried, the slaves carrying the litter and Simón riding his horse alongside. When night came, they lit torches to show them the way and rushed on.

But their efforts were in vain. No one in Caracas could help María Teresa either and on January 22, 1803, she died. She and Simón had been married just eight months. Simón was shattered. He swore that he would never get married again. Many years later he told a friend, "I loved my wife. . . . If I had not lost her, my whole life might have been different. I should not have been General Bolívar or the Liberator . . ."

He could not stay in Venezuela. Not now. Everywhere he

turned he met memories of María Teresa. So at the end of 1803, he fled back to Spain.

The second time Simón visited Paris he found it much improved.

Chapter 3

A PROMISE

Spain, Simón discovered, was no better than Venezuela. It too brought memories of María Teresa. He had to find somewhere else to go and something else to think about. In March of 1804, the Spanish government helped make a decision for him. There was not enough flour in the country, they announced. All foreigners would have to leave so the real Spaniards would not run out of bread. Of course a Creole like Simón was considered a foreigner too. So at the age of twenty, still grieving, he packed his bags and once again set out for Paris.

The city, he soon saw, had improved since his last visit. Coaches now clattered through the streets, vendors shouted their wares, and musicians entertained the passersby. Shops actually had goods to sell and restaurants and cafés offered some of the best meals he had ever tasted. A few places were even lighted by gas lamps, which made them look like fairylands.

What comforted Simón most, though, was his friendship with a distant cousin, Fanny du Villars. Fanny was about twenty-seven, the wife of a much older man who often was away on business. To amuse herself, she held "salons," gatherings in her home to which she invited some of the most interesting people in Paris. Simón soon found himself a regular guest at these salons. He also may have become more than friends with Fanny. In any case, his grief for María Teresa eased and he was able to think about the future again.

One thing was certain. He did not like everything he saw in the new Paris. The whole point of the French Revolution had been to give all citizens liberty through a government that truly represented them. From what he observed, most people had already forgotton this noble goal. All they seemed to care about was having a good time.

Then there was Napoleon, the great hero of the people, who had won Simón's admiration too. Perhaps so much glory had gone to the first consul's head. No longer could he be satisfied only with the people crying *"Vive Bonaparte!"* (Long live Bonaparte!). Now the very parrots in his home had to shout these words at him. In itself, that probably was not important. But it turned out to be a symbol of what was to come.

On May 18, 1804, Napoleon had himself proclaimed emperor of the French. For Simón that was too much. Napoleon had been his hero. Now that hero was no better than any other tyrant. Kings and queens, emperors and empresses— none of these had any place in the picture forming in Simón's mind of what a government should be.

He was not the only person to be upset by Napoleon's actions. The stormy German composer, Ludwig van Beethoven, had idolized Bonaparte too. He had even dedicated his third symphony, *The Eroica* (The Heroic), to him. But when Napoleon called himself emperor, Beethoven crossed out that dedication with a vicious slash of his pen.

About this time, Simón met the famous explorer and scientist, Alexander von Humboldt. Humboldt had been to Venezuela and had his own ideas about what was going on there. He told Simón that the country was ready for freedom. But, he asked, who will make it happen? That gave Simón something new to think about.

At last, when he felt he could not bear another day in Paris, an old friend showed up—Simón Rodríguez. He was calling himself Robinson now, after his favorite fictional character, Robinson Crusoe. A change of scene would do them both good, Simón decided. Why not a walking tour? They could rage against Napoleon all the way if they liked and see some new sights as well.

They must have made a strange pair—shabby Robinson trudging along bareheaded, the books he loved best poking out of his pockets, and dapper young Simón striding beside him. As in the old days, they had a marvelous time.

One of their first stops was a house at Chambéry where the philosopher Jean-Jacques Rousseau had lived for several years. Then they spent eleven days journeying through the

Alps and at last wound up in Italy. They got there at almost the same time as Napoleon, although the emperor's trip was much more elaborate. He had come to crown himself king of Italy and rode along flower-strewn paths in the company of a staff in fancy uniforms.

One thing about Napoleon did impress Simón, though. In spite of his staff's fine feathers, he dressed simply, which made him stand out in a way that layers of gold and embroidery never could.

In Italy, Simón and Robinson wandered from city to town. They were especially eager to see Venice, the city after which Venezuela had been named. But when they arrived, they were disappointed. Yes, Venice was beautiful. But as far as they were concerned, Venezuela was much more beautiful.

Finally they came to Rome and Simón felt his heart beat faster. To him, Rome was almost magical, the birthplace of a republic that had conquered large parts of the world. He met the pope and gazed in awe at the Colosseum. But one of the most important moments of his life took place on the Monte Sacro (Holy Mountain), a hill in the northern part of the city. He and Robinson had climbed the hill on a warm summer day. When they got to the top, they sat on a broken marble column to rest and began to talk about freedom. It was a natural topic to discuss, since two thousand years earlier, ordinary Roman people had declared on this very hill that they should have the same rights as the nobility. The sun was just setting when Simón stood up and began a speech about the history of Rome. He listed heroes and monsters, good times and bad, victories and defeats.

"Here all greatness had its pattern," he declared, "and all misery its cradle."

Then his thoughts turned to his own country. All at once the dreams that had been chasing through his head for the past several years seemed to fall into place.

"I swear before you," he cried to Robinson, "I swear before the God of my fathers; by my fathers themselves, by my honor and by my country, that my arm shall not rest nor my mind be at peace until I have broken the chains which bind me, by the will and power of Spain."

It was a promise he never forgot. Although he finished his travels through Italy with Robinson and went on to London, his heart and mind had already returned to Venezuela. That summer day on the Monte Sacro, the Liberator had been born.

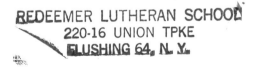

King Charles IV of Spain

Chapter 4

REVOLUTION

In February of 1807, Simón Bolívar went back to Caracas. Right away he saw that Humboldt had been wrong. The Venezuelan people were not ready yet for a revolution. They were not on fire with the same longing for independence that Simón felt.

They had shown their lack of enthusiasm just a year earlier when General Francisco de Miranda tried to start an uprising. Miranda had an incredible plan. He wanted to form one huge state that would extend from the mouth of the Mississippi in the north to Cape Horn in the south and the Pacific Ocean in the west. This would include all of Mexico and most of South America, except for Brazil and Guiana. The state would have a Parliament something like Britain's, with a House of Lords and a House of Commons. But instead of a king or queen, it would have an emperor called the inca.

Miranda had gone from the United States to England to several European countries and back to England in search of financial support for his great plan. No one was interested. At last he used his own money to hire 180 soldiers in New York. With only this tiny army and three ships, he sailed for the Venezuelan coast. Before he could land, the

Spanish attacked him, sank two of his ships, and captured sixty of his men.

But Miranda was not beaten yet. He went back to the United States, borrowed some money, and tried again. This time he landed at the port city of Coro. But, to his amazement, the city was empty. Not only did the Venezuelans not want to fight in a revolution, they did not want to be anywhere near when one was happening.

So Miranda sailed away again and went back to England. He must have taken some very bitter feelings with him. He had risked his life and his fortune to give the people freedom and in return they had said, "No, thanks."

Bolívar knew all this and was not about to make the same mistakes Miranda had. First, the people's hearts and imaginations had to be set afire. They needed ideas to believe in and leaders whom they would loyally follow. Furthermore, Simón would never get anywhere if he did not have the support of his fellow Creoles. They, after all, had more influence than anyone else in Venezuela.

So Bolívar set out to win over the Creoles. He went to their dances and parties and held some of his own. He dropped an idea here and spoke with an important person there. Bit by bit, he laid the foundations for a revolutionary movement and he did it in such a charming way that even when the Spanish suspected he was up to something, they did not take it all that seriously.

Then, in 1808, events in Europe played right into the revolutionaries' hands. Napoleon forced Charles IV to leave the throne and set up his own brother, Joseph, as king of Spain.

Oh, no you don't! cried the Spanish people. If Charles is too weak to hang onto this throne, we will form another government and make Charles's son, Ferdinand VII, our king.

England, who was fighting Napoleon and the French, also supported Ferdinand. So now Spain had two governments— the French one with Joseph and the Spanish one with Ferdinand. It was just the sort of mess that Bolívar and his friends needed.

Many South Americans said they could never support a French king. They were behind Ferdinand all the way. But Bolívar knew that Ferdinand could not do much at the moment as a king in exile. He also doubted if that crybaby, who had pouted when he got his hat knocked off, would be much of a ruler later either. So he formed a secret society, the Sociedad Patriótica (Patriotic Society) that met at his home, and went on working for revolution.

In 1810, Spain sent a new governor to Venezuela, Vicente de Emparán. Emparán was a likable man, but a strict ruler. He soon found out about Bolívar's secret society and even saw the young man drink a toast to South American independence at a banquet.

But Emparán was also a friend of the Bolívar family and did not want to arrest Simón. So he quietly suggested that

Simón go away from Caracas for a while. After thinking about it, Simón agreed.

Because of this, he missed one of the more dramatic moments of the revolution. On April 19, 1810—the Thursday before Easter—some of the revolutionaries stopped Emparán as he was entering a church and told him that he must come with them to their council chamber. When they got to the chamber, they informed Emparán that he could not be governor anymore.

Emparán, who was clever, asked, "Why not let the people decide?" He went out onto a balcony.

"Do you wish me to remain with you as governor?" he asked the crowd below.

"No!" shouted the crowd.

Emparán was too much of a gentleman to make a fuss and the rebels treated him with equal respect. They escorted him to the port at La Guaira and put him on a Spanish ship.

Just like that, Venezuela was free of Spain. The new leaders, called a *junta*, politely banished all Spanish officials and got busy setting up their own government. As their model, they copied the young government that seemed to be working so well in the United States.

Bolívar came back to Caracas and was appointed a diplomat to England, along with Luis López Méndez. Andrés Bello, one of Bolívar's former tutors, went with them. And Bolívar offered to pay for the whole trip.

In London they had to play a crafty game. England was still for Spain and against France, so the delegates were supposed to pretend to support Ferdinand. It was not long, though, before Bolívar began talking about independence. The English listened. They certainly wanted to protect Venezuela from France. But support the new government against Spain? Well, they could not do that. Spain was, after all, their ally.

Bolívar had another mission in England too, one that went against the wishes of the junta in Caracas. He wanted to bring General Miranda, who was sixty now, back to Venezuela. Such an act would completely destroy the pretense of Venezuela's loyalty to Ferdinand. The whole world knew how Miranda felt about his country's independence. But Bolívar firmly believed that Miranda was "the man the revolution wanted."

It must have been a touching moment when the handsome young rebel asked the old soldier to come home again. Miranda said yes at once. They sailed back to Venezuela in September of 1810. When they got there, Bolívar invited the general to his own home. The junta was not especially pleased with Miranda's presence, but eventually made him a lieutenant general in the army and a member of Venezuela's new congress.

On July 5, 1811, that congress published Venezuela's declaration of independence. No one was pretending anything now. The rebels had announced to all the world that Venezuela was free.

Chapter 5

FAILURE

Trouble began immediately. Of course Spain had every intention of crushing the upstart rebels. But there also were many people in Venezuela who still felt loyal to Spain. The revolution could no longer be won by parades and speeches. It was time to fight and Miranda seemed the logical person to lead the army.

Army? he asked. All he had was some simple farmers, ready to defend their country, but totally undisciplined.

Miranda, on the other hand, was a soldier of the old school. He believed in perfectly formed ranks of men, fighting together like a well-oiled machine. Bolívar and some of the other young officers tried to convince him that his men would make fine guerrilla fighters. But he would not listen. Instead, he tried to whip them into his kind of soldiers overnight. Many of them promptly responded by deserting.

In spite of these problems, Miranda's army seemed to be holding its own. Then an officer in the Spanish navy, Juan Domingo Monteverde, proved his ability to fight on land as well and won several minor battles against Miranda. Monteverde was just gearing up for a major attack when a blow fell from a completely unexpected direction.

On March 26, 1812—again the Thursday before Easter—Caracas and many other towns held by the rebels were struck by one of the worst earthquakes in history. Churches caved in, burying worshipers in the rubble. Large numbers of soldiers died right in their barracks. Bolívar's house, along with many others in Caracas, crumbled to the ground.

But instead of trying to save his possessions from looters, Simón immediately formed a group of friends and slaves and set out to help other victims in the city. Some he pulled out of the ruins and placed on stretchers until they could get medical attention. For others it was too late for medical attention and he ordered their bodies burned before disease could add to the city's problems.

Strangely enough, the earthquake did almost no damage to the camps of the soldiers who supported Spain. One of those soldiers saw Bolívar digging through the rubble and yelled out that even nature was against the rebels' cause.

"Even if Nature itself is against us," Bolívar shouted back, "we will not give in. We will fight Nature too and make it obey us."

A monk, climbing on a table in the ruins of a nearby church, began to curse Bolívar. As a crowd gathered, he preached that God was against the rebels too. The crowd, he said, should do God's will and strike Bolívar down. The people muttered and grumbled at this command and Bolívar knew that he must strike first. So he leaped up onto the table beside the monk and knocked him down with the flat of his sword. It was a daring act, but it worked. The crowd stared in shock, then, one by one, drifted away.

In spite of his personal losses, the confusion in Venezuela, and the ever-present threat of the Spanish army, Bolívar tried to urge the rebels on in the days that followed. Sometimes it must have seemed to him that his problems were insurmountable. The state of emergency was so severe that the government appointed Miranda commander-in-chief. That was about the same as naming him dictator. People who had been lukewarm to the revolution before now said they had no intention of following Miranda. Some even switched sides completely and supported the Spanish.

Furthermore, Miranda decided that he had had enough of Bolívar. He may have felt that the energetic young officer made him look bad in comparison. In any case, he sent Bolívar off to command the fort of Puerto Cabello, a tricky job to say the least.

While Bolívar was there, a Venezuelan officer went over to the Spanish side and began to attack Simón and his men. The rebels defended their position for a week, but without reinforcements they had no chance. Puerto Cabello fell and Bolívar and his remaining forty men barely got out with their lives.

Meanwhile, Miranda did have more soldiers than Monteverde, even if they were not well trained. But he dithered around, still trying to turn them into the sort of army he liked instead of sending them out to attack the enemy forces. Then, on July 11, 1812, without consulting anyone, Miranda simply gave up. Alexander Scott, a representative from the United States who had come with food for the earthquake victims, said it was "a shameful and treacherous capitulation."

According to the agreement Miranda made with the Spaniards, the rebels would not be prosecuted for their political acts. If they wished, they would be given passports to leave Venezuela. But Miranda did not even stay to make sure the Spaniards followed this agreement. He sneaked off to La Guaira and found a ship to England. He made one bad mistake, though. Instead of getting on the ship right away, he decided to spend the night ashore. There Bolívar and some other officers found him. They arrested him on the spot and put him in custody of the port commander. The next day the commander went over to the Spanish side and gave Miranda to Monteverde.

According to the terms of surrender, Monteverde had no right to touch the old man. But he knew that Miranda had a huge price on his head in Spain. So he put Miranda in chains and sent him away. For four years, Miranda sat shackled to the wall of a Spanish prison. At last he died and in a final act of cruelty, his captors threw his body into the mud.

Many years later, even the Venezuelans whom he had

failed thought this was too harsh a punishment for a man who had, after all, given a great deal to his country. They built a large tomb for Miranda in Caracas. It stands empty, but it remains a memorial to the general who believed with all his heart in Venezuela's freedom.

Since Monteverde had already ignored the terms of surrender once, he soon had no trouble forgetting them entirely. He arrested many of the rebels and shot some of them. He sent the leaders of the congress to Spain and publicly burned the constitution. He also took all property belonging to important Creoles.

That left Bolívar in a bad situation. For a while, he hid out at the home of an old family friend in Caracas. But he knew that eventually he would have to leave the country and to do that he would need a passport. The only way to get one was to talk to Monteverde. So when another friend, a man who knew Monteverde too, offered to go with him, Bolívar agreed. For a few minutes, Monteverde had his most dangerous enemy right where he wanted him. But he did not realize that. He had no idea how much Bolívar had done for the revolution—or how much he would do in the future. As far as Monteverde was concerned, he was looking at just one more silly young man. So he picked up his pen and signed the passport. Bolívar was free.

The cathedral in the background in Cartagena, Colombia, was erected by the Spanish conquerors.

Chapter 6

A NEW START

Using the precious passport, Bolívar traveled to Curaçao, an island under British rule. Monteverde had all of Bolívar's property back in Venezuela. Most of his baggage was still in a shed at La Guaira. Something had been wrong with his ship's papers, so British customs fined him and took the rest of his luggage and money. He was penniless, defeated, and worried about his family, who were in hiding somewhere. But he had no intention of giving up.

Instead, he went on to New Granada. This province, west of Venezuela, included what are now Colombia, Ecuador, and Panamá. New Granada had had its revolutions too. Parts of it still remained free of Spain, but the area as a whole was not very well organized. Each city had its own government and these governments often bickered with one another.

Bolívar settled in Cartagena, a port on the northwest coast. He thought he understood what had gone wrong with his revolution and he wanted the people of New Granada to understand too, so they would not make the same mistakes. To reach them, he wrote for the Granadan newspapers. His writings soon became known as the Manifesto of Cartagena.

The worst mistake the Venezuelan rebels made, he said, was that they did not do enough. They sat back and let things happen when they should have been busy. They could have captured Coro, but they let the Spaniards get it. Instead of solving practical problems, they discussed philosophies. Furthermore, they had pardoned far too many Spaniards and let them stay around to cause more trouble. They did not begin training their own army soon enough and they harmed Venezuela's economy by taking farm workers from the land and trying to turn them into soldiers. They spent too much money on salaries for government officials. They issued paper money, which many people thought was almost worthless. Finally, they tried to model their government too closely on that of the United States and Venezuela was not yet ready for such a government.

New Granada could not remain free, warned Bolívar, as long as Spain ruled Venezuela. He ended his manifesto with a plea: "Avenge the dead, give life to the dying, relieve the oppressed, and bring freedom to all!"

The manifesto deeply moved many New Granadans, including the governor of Cartagena and the president of the congress in Tunja. It also made good sense. So the government made Bolívar a colonel in the army and assigned him to the village of Barrancas.

Barrancas sat beside the Magdalena River, one of the most important communication routes in New Granada.

Many of the towns along the Magdalena were held by the Spanish and Bolívar could not wait to drive them out. But his orders were simply to hold the fort at Barrancas. For a few days he amused himself by having a love affair with a young peasant girl, Anita Lenoit. Soon, though, neither love nor orders could keep him from fighting a battle he knew he could win.

On the night of December 21, he and his two hundred men climbed onto ten little rafts and began to pole their way upstream. Both the darkness and the thick jungle growth along the river gave them cover as they slid through the swift-flowing water toward the town of Tenerife.

It was still dark when they tied their rafts to the river-bank and crept ashore. Guides led them along a trail through the jungle. Then, suddenly, a guard called out. Bolívar's men grabbed the guard and cut his throat, but it was too late. The other Spaniards had heard and came running. Guns blazing, Bolívar and his men chased them all the way back to Tenerife. Then the rebel army hid and Bolívar shouted to the Spanish commander that he had better surrender or Bolívar's artillery would blow up the town. Bolívar did not have any artillery. But the Spanish commander did not know that. He and his five hundred troops fled. Bolívar and his men took over both the town and the Spanish arsenal. They had not suffered one casualty.

It was a great day for Bolívar and it got even better when

Anita Lenoit slipped through his door. She had followed him all the way from her home. Flushed with victory, Bolívar held her in his arms and promised that one day he would come back and marry her. Anita waited for seventeen years. Bolívar never came.

Since the battle at Tenerife had gone so well, Bolívar felt that he must press on immediately. So the night of December 22, he and his men continued upriver to the town of Mompox. But they found no Spaniards when they got there. Word of their coming had gone before them and these Spaniards had fled too. Furthermore, three hundred men from the town announced that they wanted to join Bolívar's forces. In five days, those forces won five battles. Before long, there were no Spanish soldiers left in the province of Cartagena.

The boy who liked to dress up and parade around with his father's regiment had now become a man who understood some of the realities of making war. You did not sit back and let the enemy make the first move. And if a trick worked, you used it.

Once, when he could see no way into a Spanish fort up on a hill, Bolívar planted false information on one of his soldiers. Then he told the man to go out and wander around as if he were lost. The Spaniards caught the man, read the information, and hurried away to the place where they thought Bolívar would attack. While they were gone, Bolívar and his men simply marched up the hill and took over their fort.

Another time, he sent a small force after the Spaniards in a town they held. This little group struck, then pulled back at once. The Spaniards, sure of victory, poured out of their fortified town to crush the rebels. The moment they were in the open, Bolívar attacked them with his main force and soundly defeated them.

By using his imagination to devise tactics such as these, Bolívar was able to get the most out of his army and win time and again over larger, better-equipped Spanish forces.

At last he reached the border between New Granada and Venezuela. Now it was time to put his most important plan into action, to push ahead all the way to Caracas.

Bolívar knew he looked good in his uniform and he enjoyed parading around.

Chapter 7

VICTORY!

The soldiers who followed Bolívar both loved and respected him. This was partly due to the fact that he led them from one victory to another. But there was more to it than that. Bolívar was an officer who was not afraid to get his hands dirty. When his men sweltered in the hot sun, he sweltered with them. If they had to trudge through mud up to their knees, he trudged through it too.

Bolívar also knew how to talk to his men, to cheer them on when they were ready to drop with exhaustion and to praise them for their accomplishments. At the Venezuelan border, he called them brave heroes and told them that South America expected freedom to come from them.

Unfortunately, not all of Bolívar's officers were as responsive as the men. Some were frankly jealous of Bolívar's achievements. Others could see no reason why they, New Granadans, should have to follow a Venezuelan into battle in *his* home country.

But the congress at Tunja, which had given Bolívar his command in the first place, thought differently. They were delighted with all he had done. To reward him—and to give him the power he would need—they made him an honorary citizen of New Granada, promoted him to the rank of brigadier general, and told him to go ahead with his plan to move into Venezuela.

Even then, some of Bolívar's officers grumbled, especially Francisco de Paula Santander. In fact, Santander stated flatly that he would not advance. Furious, Bolívar pointed his pistol at the man and gave him an ultimatum. If he did not march at once, he could try to shoot Bolívar. But chances were very good that Bolívar would shoot him first. Santander marched.

The Venezuela Bolívar entered was a much sadder place than it had been when he left. Monteverde, who had more or less appointed himself Spain's representative through his military victories, had decided to govern the fallen nation by the "law of conquest." This meant that he and his men could do anything they wanted—no matter how bloodthirsty or reprehensible—because they were the victors. Creoles, in particular, were shot left and right. If a man even was suspected of sympathizing with the rebels, he and his entire family could be put to death. Needless to say, prisoners of war did not stand a chance; they were executed on the spot.

The revolutionaries, on the other hand, had preferred to fight more like gentlemen. The prisoners they captured had remained alive. No more, though, announced Bolívar. It was time they met Monteverde on his own terms. From now on, his men would fight a "war to the death" also.

Civilized countries have frowned on such a policy for centuries. The truth was that Bolívar did not like it either. In more than one situation in the days ahead, he would ignore it. But he felt he needed the threat of "war to the death" to fight Monteverde effectively.

One by one, he piled up victories. Mérida. Trujillo. San Carlos. Valencia. Other officers fought valiantly in other places. Ribas won brilliantly at Niquitao and Los Horcones. Arismendi recaptured the island of Margarita. Mariño, Bermúdez, Piar, and Sucre all did their parts. In ninety-three days, Bolívar swept across the six hundred miles between the Venezuelan border and Caracas. By August of 1813, he was ready to enter the city.

The Spaniard in charge in Caracas, Manuel del Fierro, must have been shaking in his boots. Here this Bolívar fellow had started out from New Granada with a mere two hundred men. True, he had picked up another six hundred along the way. Even so, it was a tiny army and yet it had managed to rout some six thousand Spaniards. What sort of man *was* this Simón Bolívar?

For one thing, he was a man who really did not like the policy of "war to the death." He immediately assured Fierro that he did not plan to shoot people, arrest them, take their property, or get even with them in any way. As far as he was concerned, the sooner people were reconciled, the better off everyone would be.

Such generosity, thought Fierro, was too good to be true. Therefore, it probably was not true. He agreed to the peace treaty. Then he and some six thousand of his supporters fled to La Guaira.

All this happened while Bolívar was still at La Victoria, outside Caracas. No doubt he was well aware that just a year earlier, General Miranda had surrendered to Monteverde in this very place. But the time had come to put those gloomy thoughts behind him. His golden moment had arrived, the moment when he would ride triumphantly into his home city.

First Bolívar changed clothes. Out on the battlefield, he let himself get as grubby as his men, but now he would shine in a blue and white uniform, trimmed with gold. He would ride a white stallion too, instead of the mule he used for fighting.

His tired, proud men marching behind him, he reached the bridge that spanned the Guaire River. Stretching across the bridge was an arch made of flowers with a huge crowd of people gathered under it. He must get off his horse, a committee informed him, and ride in the chariot they had specially prepared for him. His eyes glowing, Bolívar climbed into the chariot. Then twelve young girls picked up a silken rope and pulled him all the way into Caracas. Church bells rang and cannon roared. Bands played and the crowds cheered until they were hoarse.

In the city itself, still more people hung over rooftops or from balconies to toss flowers down on the heroes. Others mobbed them in the streets, hugging, kissing, and sometimes crying. Prison doors were flung open and former revolutionaries burst from their cells to join the throng.

All night long, Caracas celebrated with fireworks and dancing in the streets. Someone gave a ball for Bolívar and he danced all night too. Officially now he was known as the Liberator, a title that meant more to him than any he ever received. It was all perfectly glorious and he loved every moment of it.

But even in the midst of the revelry, he must have found time for a few quiet thoughts. Some of these thoughts would have been prayers of thanksgiving, because that night he was able to have dinner in his old home with his sisters and his beloved nurses, Hipólita and Matea. But other thoughts might have been concerns for the future. Caracas was his now. What was the best thing he could do for it?

Under the leadership of José Boves, the llaneros from the south turned against Bolívar.

Chapter 8

A MONSTER

Caracas, Bolívar knew, was little more than an island of peace in the middle of a sea of trouble. Fierro had surrendered, but at Puerto Cabello, Monteverde still lurked, waiting for reinforcements from Spain before he pounced. His position by the sea meant that these reinforcements could easily link up with him. It also gave him a clear channel to supplies from Puerto Rico.

At the same time, some of the New Granadan officers still nursed their jealousy of Bolívar and bombarded their government with complaints. But the worst danger of all would come from the hot, muggy south where José Tomás Boves was putting together his "Legion of Hell."

Bolívar decided to tend to first things first and set out to see what he could do about Puerto Cabello. He could not lay siege to the town because of its open harbor. But he and his men could conduct little raids and skirmishes here and there. During one of these, they captured a Spanish officer called Zuazola.

Zuazola was a particularly cruel man who liked to wear the ears of dead rebels on his hat. In spite of this, Bolívar offered to exchange him and four other Spanish prisoners for a rebel colonel. Monteverde refused. In fact, he said, from now on, he would shoot two rebel prisoners for every Spanish one who died. So Bolívar hanged Zuazola. But he went on offering other exchanges—two Spanish prisoners for every rebel. Monteverde continued to say no.

Twelve hundred Spanish reinforcements arrived via Puerto Rico and the rebels fought on. One of Bolívar's bravest young officers was a New Granadan called Girardot. On September 30, he died in battle and a corps of New Granadans set out to avenge his death. They struck a hard blow at the Spanish and shot Monteverde through the jaw. But a Colonel Salomon immediately took the fallen commander's place.

Bolívar was determined, though, that Girardot not be forgotten. He said that September 30 must always be a day of mourning in Venezuela. He sent the young man's body back to his home and promised that his family and heirs would receive his salary forever. But he had Girardot's heart removed from his body and placed in a gilded urn. This urn was then carried in a long, solemn funeral procession to Caracas and placed in a crypt by the cathedral altar. Bolívar himself spoke at the requiem mass.

On October 14, 1813, the Caracas city council appointed Bolívar captain-general of the army. In effect, this made him a dictator. He said that he did not want the office—all he wanted was to lead his forces against the enemy. Besides, he said, a country where one man has all the power is a land of slaves. At the same time, he knew that Venezuela desperately needed order and stability. So he agreed to rule until these things were accomplished and elections could be held.

Meanwhile, the Spanish army continued to grow. Bolívar had little time to sit back in Caracas and think about his new government. He had to go out and fight one battle after another. After an especially glorious victory, officials called a popular assembly in Caracas and said again that they wanted Bolívar to serve as dictator—only this time they used the actual word. Once again he protested, but in the end still agreed to keep his office.

While all this was happening in Caracas, a terrible menace was emerging in the south. There stretched the llanos on which lived wild cattle and horses. The llaneros were almost as wild as the animals they were supposed to herd and tame. Most of the llaneros were slaves, but their owners lived far away and had little to do with their daily lives. The llaneros spent their days on horseback. For food they killed cattle, dried the meat in the sun, and cut it into strips. They kept these strips under their saddles as they rode and eventually their horses' sweat salted the meat. Then the llaneros ate it.

These men did not care in the least about politics or what happened anywhere else. All that mattered to them was their own world and in that world, physical strength was the most important quality anyone could possess. Bolívar had ridden with the llaneros for a while when he was a boy and had had a marvelous time. Now, though, thanks to the devilish leadership of José Tomás Boves, the llaneros were about to turn against him.

Boves had been both a pirate and a smuggler. Then the Spanish caught him and sent him away to Calabozo, a town in the llanos. There he became a storekeeper. He was an average-sized man with a big head, red hair, blue eyes, and a sharp nose. He would have nothing to do with alcohol, tobacco, or women. His one vice was violence—especially torture—and he excelled at it.

Boves began his military career with the revolutionaries. But one day an officer struck him for some misconduct. Boves was furious. He vowed vengeance and switched to the Spanish side. For a while he fought under Monteverde, but when the commander retired with his wound, Boves headed back to the llanos and began to put together his own army. It was not hard. He simply told the llaneros that their job was to fight for him. In return, whenever they took a town they could have all the women and loot they wanted. He, Boves, would be satisfied if he could torture and kill the men and children. The only people they would both spare were surgeons and musicians. Boves knew that even llaneros needed someone to tend their wounds. They also liked to hear a cheerful tune sometimes.

This sounded like a fine deal to the llaneros and Boves's army grew quickly. By the time he attacked his own hometown, Calabozo, he had seven thousand men with him. Even some of the Spanish were horrified and sickened by the things this army did. It was the Spanish who gave Boves's men the name "Legion of Hell." But a few Spanish officers chose to admire the monstrous acts and began to devise new brands of torture of their own.

Back in Caracas, Bolívar was facing enemy forces from almost every direction. Spanish reinforcements continued to pour into Puerto Cabello. Rosette, one of Boves's admirers, was cutting a bloody swathe from the east. And from the south, Boves himself crept closer and closer.

When the Spanish prisoners at La Guaira tried to break out, Bolívar told the commander to execute every last one of them. He told the commander in charge of prisoners at Caracas the same thing. Hundreds of prisoners died. It was one of the few situations in which Bolívar actually followed the "war to the death" policy, but at this point he was desperate.

On February 28, 1814, Boves and Bolívar met in battle at Bolívar's estate, San Mateo. Everything was destroyed. A Colombian captain, Ricaurte, had been put in charge of defending the sugar mill where the ammunition was stored. He soon saw that his situation was hopeless and ordered his men to retreat. Then he blew up the mill—and himself. In later years, the rest of San Mateo would be rebuilt. But the sugar mill remained in ruins as a memorial to Ricaurte.

In the days that followed Bolívar lost more and more battles. Each loss must have been an agony to him because he knew how Boves would treat the townspeople. When Boves took Valencia, he held a ball and stood there with a whip, forcing the women to dance while in a nearby field his llaneros drove their lances through the men.

At last Bolívar decided to evacuate Caracas. He and his forces, plus some thirty thousand civilians, marched 150 miles to a town near the coast. Many of the civilians died before they got there. The survivors finally found their way to the island of Margarita or to the British West Indies.

In a last attempt, Bolívar joined forces with another officer, Mariño. But even their two armies could not withstand the "Legion of Hell." On June 15, 1814, they fell and the second republic of Venezuela died.

Now it seemed as if Boves would have everything his own way. From city to city he traveled, torturing, mutilating, and killing as he went. His own commanding officer complained to Spain about him. But officials in Spain replied that Boves was doing a good job.

Finally, in December, a young black soldier plunged a lance into Boves at the battle of Urica. The monster died and his enemies were not the only ones who rejoiced.

Chapter 9

JEALOUSY

Once again Bolívar returned to Cartagena in New Granada. This time he was completely alone. Not one soldier came with him. But the people of New Granada did not blame him for his defeat. Instead, they gave him a hero's welcome and invited him to stay in one of the city's palaces.

But Bolívar traveled on to Tunja. He felt he must stand before the congress as a prisoner would and explain what he had done and what had gone wrong. The congress would not hear of any such thing. They gave him an ovation and the president, Camilo Torres, invited Bolívar to sit beside him.

"General," he said, "your country is not dead while your sword is still alive."

Bolívar still wanted to explain. One of his worst problems had been jealousy among his officers. Many of them simply would not cooperate with him or with one another. If they had managed to work together, Venezuela's second republic might not have failed.

The congress accepted Bolívar's explanations and made him commander-in-chief. Obviously they still had faith in him. But even their faith was not enough to weed out the jealousy that continued to grow among some New Granadan officers—and that would ultimately bring tragedy to New Granada too.

At this time, the Spaniards held only one city in New Granada, the port of Santa Marta. But there were problems in Bogotá where a rebel, Manuel Alvarez, had made himself dictator. The congress wanted Bolívar to overthrow Alvarez and bring Bogotá back under their control. Bolívar could see their point. But he didn't like the idea of fighting against a fellow rebel, even if the man had turned himself into a dictator.

Still, he took the troops the congress gave him and marched off. He and his men had almost reached Bogotá when Alvarez asked the Spanish to fight with him. That solved Bolívar's problem. He owed no loyalty to anyone who would ask for Spanish help. He captured Bogotá in just three days. A grateful congress promptly moved their headquarters to the city and put Bolívar in charge of all troops in New Granada.

It was time, the congress knew, to drive the Spanish out of Santa Marta too. If they waited, fresh forces might arrive from Spain and make the job more difficult, if not impossible. So they told Bolívar to go back to Cartagena, pick up the remaining troops and equipment there, and then proceed to Santa Marta.

Again Bolívar obeyed. But before he even reached Cartagena, he ran into the same old problem that had been bedeviling him for years. Manuel del Castillo, commander of the Cartagena forces, refused to cooperate. He would not, he declared, give up either his men or his equipment.

Quickly Bolívar sent a message to President Torres, telling him about Castillo's attitude. Torres wrote back at once. Bolívar was in charge of all troops, he said, and that included Castillo and his men. So Bolívar tried to reason with Castillo. He offered to negotiate with the jealous commander. He promoted him to brigadier general. Castillo would not budge. Then Bolívar himself tried to resign. The congress would not let him.

Five months passed during which New Granada could have been building up strong defenses against Spain. Instead, her commander-in-chief had to waste time pandering to the ego of an insubordinate officer. Bolívar knew that a direct attack on Cartagena would not do any good. The city was too well fortified and he did not have the proper equipment. Also, he still did not want to have to fight against fellow rebels. So he kept on trying to reason with Castillo and at the same time lay siege to the city.

Neither tactic worked. Castillo refused to listen to reason and the area around the city was so unhealthy that Bolívar's men began to die from smallpox and tropical fever. At last Bolívar gave up in disgust. He resigned—and this time he meant it. On June 9, 1815, he sailed away to the British island of Jamaica. Many New Granadans were upset by his leaving. Many more would share those feelings in the days and months ahead.

For some time now, events in Europe had been coming together in ways that would forever change the face and the future of South America. They began in April of 1814 when Napoleon was defeated and his brother, Joseph, pulled off the Spanish throne. By that June day in 1815 when Bolívar set sail for Jamaica, Ferdinand VII was firmly in control of Spain and ready to deal with those troublesome colonies in the New World.

Ferdinand's plan was simple. He had plenty of experienced troops who no longer had to fight Napoleon. So he would send fifteen thousand of them to South America with orders to crush even the faintest whisper of revolution. General Pablo Morillo was in charge of these troops and he carried out Ferdinand's orders to the letter. His purges began in Venezuela. To many it seemed as if Monteverde had returned.

When Morillo met Colonel Morales, who had taken over the llaneros after Boves's death, he gave the half-naked cowboys a long, scornful look. Then he informed Morales that they should either be disciplined or disbanded. Morales replied that if anyone tried either procedure on the llaneros, they would switch over to the rebel side. Morillo could not see why either side would want them.

Before long, Morillo and his forces were attacking Cartagena by sea while Morales attacked it by land. The city held for 106 days, but inside its walls the people were dying from starvation, thirst, and disease. They ate every living thing they could find and even dug in the ground for ants and grubs. At last about two thousand of them tried to escape in small boats. Not many made it.

The Spanish poured into the city and found three hundred more survivors. Although most of them were close to death already, the soldiers marched them out to the beach and beheaded them. One of the three hundred was Manuel del Castillo. He had paid a heavy price for his jealousy.

With Cartagena laid waste, there was nothing to stop the Spanish army from moving up the Magdalena River to Bogotá. The congress, with no one to defend it, said that the city would surrender if the Spanish would promise amnesty. The Spanish promised. Then they marched in and immediately executed six hundred people, including President Camilo Torres.

Meanwhile, safe in Jamaica, Bolívar felt like a caged animal. He lived in a small, bare hut—penniless again. He even had to borrow money from an English friend to pay a woman to wash his one shirt. During the day he paced back and forth and wrote letters. At night he slept in a hammock or slipped away to have love affairs with various women.

One night, while he was at the home of one of his mistresses, a friend came to the hut to visit him. When he saw that Bolívar was not there, he lay down in the hammock to wait for his return. As the hours passed, he must have fallen asleep. The next morning, his body was found. He had been stabbed twice, once in the throat and once in the heart. The murderer turned out to be Bolívar's servant. Two Spanish men had paid him two thousand pesos to kill his employer. In the dark, he had not realized that the man in the hammock was not Bolívar.

Apparently the Spaniards felt they would not be safe from Bolívar until he was dead. They were right. But at the moment, his most powerful weapon was his pen. Among the many letters he wrote while he was in Jamaica was one as long as a small book. It was similar to the Manifesto of Cartagena that he had written after the fall of the first republic of Venezuela. In the Jamaica Letter, he talked about the past, present, and future of South America.

Spain, he said, would never be able to conquer—and hold—the colonies. There were not enough forces in the whole country to do that. The rest of Europe should try to talk the Spanish out of such a foolish plan. In fact, the rest of Europe should have thought of South America's independence long ago. It would definitely be to their advantage economically because independent South American nations would be able to trade with whomever they liked.

On the other hand, Bolívar explained, the countries of South America were not ready for a federal republic style of government like that of the United States. The people's culture, customs, and temperament were just too different.

He went on to list the sort of government that would probably work best in each country. (In most cases, history has proved him right.) Then he talked about his own dearest dream. He wanted the various countries of Central and South America to form a sort of union or congress. Its purpose would not be to govern, but to meet with the other nations of the world—in Panamá—to discuss questions of war and peace.

Bolívar knew that such a congress could not happen right away. But it was one of the shining hopes for the future that kept him going. His Jamaica Letter was published for people all over the world to read and many of them were struck by its wisdom and farsightedness.

Meanwhile, though, the author of that letter still lived in poverty and exile on a British island. Each batch of fresh news plunged him into greater sadness, as the Spanish systematically erased every victory he had won. In all, he would spend six months in Jamaica. Then help would come from three very different people.

Top: Bolívar on horseback leading his troops in battle

Bottom left: Ferdinand VII, king of Spain

Bottom right: Spanish General Pablo Morillo was sent to South America to crush the revolution.

Some of Bolívar's officers included José de San Martín (left), Francisco de Paula Santander (bottom left), and Antonio José de Sucre (bottom right).

Above: Bolívar and his generals meet to discuss the campaign of the Andes.

Below: San Martín crossing the Andes

Above: José Antonio Páez and his llaneros forces
Below: General Francisco de Miranda and Bolívar lead the signing of the
Venezuelan declaration of independence.

Above: Bolívar's summer house in Bogotá

Right: An equestrian statue of Simón Bolívar stands in Plaza Bolívar in Caracas.

Bolívar's tomb in Caracas

Alexandre Pétion, the president of Haiti

Chapter 10

UNEXPECTED HELP

While he was still in Jamaica, Bolívar received a letter from a businessman called Luis Brión. Although Brión lived on the island of Curaçao, he cared passionately about South American independence. In fact, he had just bought a 24-gun ship, full of supplies and equipment. Could he and his ship, he wondered, be of help to Bolívar?

Bolívar wrote back at once to say yes. But time passed and he heard no more from Brión. At last he could no longer bear sitting in exile. He borrowed money from a friend and chartered a little boat to take him to New Granada. At least there he might be able to do something.

At sea, though, he met up with another ship and heard the latest news. Cartagena had fallen and refugees were headed for Aux Cayes, a port on the island of Haiti. All right, declared Bolívar, Haiti it would be. He ordered his boat to change course immediately.

His arrival at Aux Cayes was the first happy moment he had experienced in a long time. There, waiting at the wharf, was Luis Brión. Apparently he had left before he received Bolívar's letter. Bolívar also met a wealthy English merchant, Robert Sutherland, who wanted to help him.

Best of all, though, Alexandre Pétion, the president of Haiti, came forward with an offer. Except for the United States, Haiti was the only free republic in the Western Hemisphere. The black citizens of this tiny nation had won their freedom from France in 1804. They despised the idea of slavery in any form and were willing to do all they could to abolish it.

They began by giving a warm welcome—not to mention food and shelter—to the thousands of South American refugees who flooded their shores. By the time Bolívar arrived, President Pétion had read the Jamaica Letter and realized that this was a man whose ideals Haiti could support. So he promised Bolívar both money and arms. In return, Bolívar promised to free Venezuela's slaves.

It was not a difficult promise for Bolívar to make. He, too, had come to hate the whole idea of slavery and had already freed those belonging to his family. A country without slaves, he believed, was far healthier than one that held on to that cruel institution. It might take a while to rid Venezuela of slavery, but he would do his best.

So with the help of those three different men—Brión, Sutherland, and Pétion—Bolívar began to think about mounting a new attack on the Spaniards who held his homeland captive. Actually, he was receiving help from a fourth person, too, and was well aware of the fact.

Ferdinand VII had made many promises to the South

Americans who agreed to uphold the Spanish throne. He was now in the process of breaking every one of those promises and his blanket cruelty to the colonies served to unite them in ways the rebels' parades and speeches never could. That same cruelty did nothing for Ferdinand's image with the rest of the world either and eventually Bolívar would find sympathy and help coming from sources far away.

Meanwhile, though, he had to put together an army. Among the refugees he discovered both soldiers and officers. Some of the officers were men who had proved their loyalty to him again and again. Others still carried the bitter poisons of jealousy and disunity with them. Never mind, thought Bolívar. He would do what he could with what he had.

The little army that finally set sail from Haiti on March 31, 1816, consisted of 250 men, arms for 4,000 men, a bit of artillery, and 7 ships. Its goal was the island of Margarita, part of which the stubborn Arismendi had taken back from the Spanish.

The moment he landed, Bolívar announced that Venezuela was once more independent and that all the slaves in the nation were free. He also said that he would abandon the "war to the death" policy if the Spanish would behave with less cruelty.

In spite of Bolívar's pathetically weak position, Morillo, head of the Spanish forces, took him seriously. He would not change his methods, he said, but he would give a reward of ten thousand pesos to the person who brought him Bolívar's head.

Bolívar began his campaign with the same fiery enthusiasm he brought to everything he did. It was not long, though, before he found himself facing the same enemy that would haunt him throughout his life—the bickering and insubordination of his own officers. This time Mariño, Piar, and Bermúdez gave him the most trouble. Bermúdez even threatened him with a sword. Bolívar knew that he could not fight the Spanish while mutiny was going on in his own camp. So he boarded a ship and returned to Haiti.

He stayed there only two months. Brión, Sutherland, and President Pétion all insisted that he must try again. Arismendi patiently recaptured Margarita and begged Bolívar to come back. To these pleas were added more from a group of officers who clearly saw how much they needed the general's leadership. Bolívar sighed and set sail.

Again the battles began. Bermúdez swore that he was sorry and promised to serve Bolívar faithfully in the future. For a long time he kept that promise. But Mariño continued to grumble and scheme. So did Piar. Piar was a brave and clever officer, but he simply could not obey orders. One of the many he disobeyed was Bolívar's strict command that prisoners must not be shot. In out-and-out defiance, Piar shot over a hundred prisoners and Bolívar knew he must act.

He first told Piar to return at once to Haiti. Piar said he would not go. So Bolívar had him up for court-martial on charges of insubordination, sedition, and desertion. The council found him guilty and sentenced him to death. A second council reviewed the actions of the first and agreed. With tears in his eyes, Bolívar signed the death sentence and the next afternoon Piar was shot. Although Bolívar hated to do such a thing, he realized that it was absolutely necessary. At least for a while now, his other officers would accept the fact that he was truly in charge.

On they fought, from town to town, always moving toward Caracas. At last they reached Angostura (today called Ciudad Bolívar). It was not a large city, but its location on the Orinoco River gave it strategic importance. It also was a good place for Bolívar and his men to catch their breath and reorganize.

Lately Bolívar had been hearing rumors about an unusual man called José Antonio Páez. He was a rebel whom the llaneros considered one of themselves and he had been giving the Spanish a great deal of trouble. All in all, he sounded like just the sort of man Bolívar needed. So he invited Páez to become one of his officers, which turned out to be a very wise move.

Páez was short with a large head, a chest like a barrel, and small, bowed legs. He looked—and was—right at home on a horse. He was born near the llanos and grew up on a cattle ranch where he soon earned the respect of everyone who knew him—including the llaneros.

At the start of the revolution, the Spanish told him that he would either fight for them or die. That was not the right thing to say to Páez. The first chance he got, he deserted, formed his own group of llaneros, and began guerrilla warfare against the Spaniards. He and his men knew their way through the llanos and usually traveled by night. They were fierce as tigers in battle, especially Páez. He had just one problem. When he got too excited or too angry, he could fall into an epileptic seizure, which kept him helpless until it had passed. His men made a point of watching out for these seizures on the battlefield. When one occurred, they scooped Páez up and carried him to safety.

After Boves was killed, many of his llaneros found their way into Páez's ranks. Soon Páez had over ten thousand troops and the Spanish had to take him very seriously— including Morillo who had once been scornful of those undisciplined llaneros.

"Those men were not a scanty band of cowards," he wrote to Ferdinand, ". . . but organized troops, able to compete with the best in Your Majesty's service."

When Páez and Bolívar first met, they embraced. That was the custom. But both felt a bit edgy. It was only when Páez saw how well Bolívar handled and cared for his horse that he decided this was a man he could follow. Once the llaneros knew their leader's feelings, they too were willing to support Bolívar.

Help was about to come from another source too. Luis López Méndez, the man with whom Bolívar had traveled to England years before, was still in London and received word that his old friend needed men. He borrowed money and held out all sorts of promises to those who would cross the ocean and fight for South American independence. His timing was perfect. Napoleon's defeat had left many trained soldiers in England and Ireland without jobs or much hope of jobs in a depressed economy. Some from Italy, Germany, and France were interested also. While a few believed in the ideals Bolívar was fighting for, most frankly needed the work.

In all, some seven or eight thousand men signed up. Many wore beautiful uniforms and quite a few even brought their wives and children with them. They had been promised land grants when the fighting was over and thought they might as well come prepared to settle down.

In a large number of cases, these promises were never fulfilled. One ship sank in a storm not far from the English coast. The others made it across the ocean, but left their passengers on various islands off the South American coast. There the foreigners heard terrible stories about Venezuela and the tyrant Bolívar. While they waited for the funds and provisions they needed to complete their journey, epidemics of typhus, yellow fever, smallpox, and other diseases claimed many lives.

Eventually, though, some of the forces managed to join up with Páez and Bolívar. Páez was especially enchanted by them, both because they were good horsemen and because they wore such splendid uniforms. He gave wild, llanero-style parties for them and in return, they taught him how to eat with a knife and fork.

Meanwhile, of course, there was fighting to be done and in spite of the reinforcements, it was not going well. An outsider might have thought that Bolívar did not know what he was doing as he took one small army after another and tried unsuccessfully to batter his way to Caracas. He rarely won and sometimes barely escaped with his own life.

But Bolívar had a plan—a brilliant plan—and he was just biding his time now until the moment came when he could put that plan into operation.

Chapter 11

A CONSTITUTION AND A CAMPAIGN

Bolívar knew that there was one more thing he must do before executing his brilliant plan. He must establish a government for Venezuela, complete with laws and a constitution. Only then would the rest of the world realize that this new republic should be taken seriously. So in February of 1819, he called together a congress at Angostura.

Not all provinces were able to send representatives. Some were still under Spanish control, but those problems could be worked out later. The important thing was to get something on paper.

Bolívar had a long speech prepared for the congress. He knew the sort of constitution he thought Venezuela should have—and why. A democracy, such as that of the United States, would not work, he said. The people could not handle it and would end up crushed by a foreign power again. But some elements of democracy could—and should—be included. For example, land should be divided fairly among the people. Taxes should be reasonable. All men aged twenty-one and over should be allowed to vote for representatives to the government. There must be freedom of religion and slavery must be abolished.

Other elements of Bolívar's proposed constitution were not as democratic. The president, although elected by the people, would serve for life. Representatives in the lower house also would be chosen by popular vote, but those in the upper house would pass their office on to their children. Congress would choose five judges for a Supreme Court as the third branch of government, but the fourth branch was uniquely Bolívar's idea. He thought there should be a group of men who would educate and supervise the morals of the rest of the government.

Most of all, though, Bolívar wanted a nation that would be unified—one republic instead of a loose federation. The past few years had shown him how desperately important it was for Venezuelans to think of themselves as one nation.

"Our slogan should be Unity, Unity, Unity," he said.

The congress altered several of Bolívar's suggestions before they adopted the new constitution. When they had finished, the president would be elected for just four years and membership in the upper house would not be hereditary. That fourth branch of government—the "censors"—was entirely abandoned. But the members of the congress thoroughly agreed with Bolívar's emphasis on unity and declared the new union of provinces "one and indivisible." They also elected Bolívar president.

Meanwhile, he had plenty to keep him busy along with setting up a government. For one thing, his armies had to be fed, clothed, and sheltered, which was not easy in a land that had been torn apart by war for so long.

One of Bolívar's favorite officers was Colonel James Rooke, a big, blond man who had come over with some of the earliest British soldiers. One night, Rooke and his pretty young wife arrived at a ball in Angostura. Bolívar took one look at the couple and his eyes opened wide. Rooke was wearing his uniform jacket all right. But under it, his chest was bare.

When Bolívar asked him the reason, Rooke grinned. He had sold his only shirt, he said, to buy a duck for dinner. Bolívar grinned too then, and sent for his servant. He would give Rooke one of his own shirts. Sorry, sir, the servant told him. You have only two shirts yourself. One is being laundered and you are wearing the other. No doubt Rooke had a fine time at the ball anyway. Bolívar always gave good parties—and plenty of them.

At last, though, the time came to begin setting his brilliant plan into motion. He announced what he would do at a banquet. Dressed in his fanciest uniform, he jumped onto the table and marched the whole length of it, glass crunching and wine splattering beneath his feet. He would cross from the Atlantic to the Pacific and from Panamá to Cape Horn, he declared, until the last Spaniard had been thrown out of South America.

His fellow guests must have thought that he was being very dramatic and inspiring. They did not realize that he meant exactly what he said. He intended to lead his army across the plains and over the Andes mountains. They would then attack the Spanish forces in New Granada and liberate the city of Bogotá. Furthermore, they would do all this during the rainy season when no one would expect it.

It was a brilliant plan all right—and a dangerous one. The army set out on February 27, 1819. But it was not until May 23, when the rains had come in earnest, that Bolívar told his officers exactly where they were headed. When he finished, they stared at him and at one another, shocked into silence.

Then Rooke cried, "Sire, I for one will follow you, even to Cape Horn."

That brought the others around and two days later the march began. In all there were twenty-four hundred soldiers, horses, mules, and cattle for food, and several hundred women—wives, other relatives, and mistresses. In those days it was not unusual for women to march off to war with their men. But this group faced an especially grueling ordeal. The difficulties began long before they reached the Andes. Heavy rains poured down on them and flooded the plains. Often the water reached up to their waists and they had to hold their belongings over their heads. The ground beneath their feet was thick, slimy mud. Leeches sucked the blood from their bodies, caribe fish tore at their flesh, and all around them lurked the silent threat of alligators. Before long, their shoes and clothing rotted away.

For three weeks they slogged along. Then they reached a tiny village called Tame on the lower slopes of the Andes. Bolívar allowed them three days there to rest. Then they began to climb. Five days later, all their horses were gone— lame or utterly exhausted.

"Just a little farther," Bolívar urged his people. Already it seemed as if he had been saying that forever.

Eventually the air grew cold and icy mists wrapped themselves around the half-naked climbers. Many of them had never experienced cold before. It felt like pain. As the air thinned, their hearts began to pound. Then came hail, sleet, and snow. In six days, they climbed thirteen thousand feet. All of the animals died and hundreds of people froze or starved to death, fell into one of the bottomless ravines, or died from "mountain sickness."

On the worst night of all, still more died, including a woman and all her children. But that same night, another woman gave birth to a baby and the next morning she stood up, held it tightly against her, and marched on. From then on, their path led downhill and soon the sad little army of scarecrows reached a sunny valley, full of flowers. People from the village of Socha took one look at them and ran for food. These scarecrows were the liberators and they would be made very welcome.

Three days' rest, decreed Bolívar, and then they would march on to battle. Between July 10 and July 15, they faced three smaller battles. In a way, the Spanish must have seemed kinder enemies than nature had been. Losses were heavy on both sides, though, when they met on July 25 and only an evening thunderstorm called a halt to the bloodbath. Among the wounded was Colonel James Rooke, who lay in a shelter made of cowhides, his fellow officers gathered around him while a doctor cut off his arm. During this terrible surgery, he grinned and made little jokes and after it was over, he said, "Viva la Patria!" (Long live the homeland!)

"Which one?" asked the doctor. "You have both English and Irish blood."

"I mean the land I'm dying for." Rooke spoke softly. He was not joking now. A few days later, he died.

"Venezuela . . . will hereafter have to attribute her liberty mainly to him," Bolívar wrote to young Mrs. Rooke, who was waiting back in Angostura.

Actually, the battle turned out to be as good as a victory for his army, because it gave them a chance to get between the Spanish soldiers and Bogotá. On August 6, the two forces met at Boyacá, with Bolívar's men surrounding the Spaniards. Not only did the enemy surrender, but when the Spanish viceroy at Bogotá heard the news, he ran away and left his whole treasury, plus a great many military supplies, behind.

On August 19, Bolívar rode into the city, a victor. He had made one of the most difficult marches in military history and then conquered an army three times as large as his own.

The city went mad. Once again he and his men traveled through flower-strewn streets, kissed by young girls and hailed as heroes by all. A couple of officers took some men and chased the remaining Spaniards from the country and at last New Granada was free.

The Battle of Carabobo, the final victory for Venezuela's independence

Chapter 12

CHAIN OF VICTORIES

On December 17, 1819, Bolívar fulfilled one of his greatest ambitions. From Angostura he published the "fundamental law of the Republic of Colombia." This meant that Venezuela and New Granada were now one state, divided into three departments: Venezuela, Quito (today's Ecuador), and Cundinamarca (today's Colombia). Of course much of this area still remained under Spanish control. But Bolívar felt certain that this would not be the case for long.

About this time, Ferdinand began having troubles at home in Spain. These troubles, plus Bolívar's successes in New Granada, caused the king to order his commander, Morillo, to negotiate with the rebels in the colonies. Bolívar and Morillo met in November of 1820. After warm words and much embracing, they decided on a six-month truce.

"It was an advantage to us, fatal to the Spaniards," said Bolívar later. "Their forces could only diminish, mine augment and organize."

Augment and organize he did, even though the truce did not last six months. But by the time war broke out again, Bolívar's army was larger and much more strategically placed. Morillo soon resigned and returned to Spain. His

89

replacement, La Torre, was not nearly as clever a commander as Morillo had been.

Bolívar wanted to meet the Spanish forces on the plain of Carabobo. In some ways the Spanish had the best position on this battlefield. But poor strategy led to their downfall. In little over an hour the fighting had finished and Bolívar found himself victorious again. He rode straight on to Caracas where the Spanish promptly surrendered. Venezuela, too, was now free.

Instead of enjoying his victories, though, Bolívar spent a great deal of time worrying. Although he was president of the new Republic of Colombia, he could not both stay at home to govern and go out to win more battles. He had already made Santander vice-president of New Granada. Now he put Páez in charge of Venezuela. Neither man was an ideal choice, but he felt they were the best he could do.

"Believe me, Gual," he wrote to a friend, "We are . . . on the top of a volcano ready for eruption. I fear peace more than war."

Worried as he was, though, Bolívar could hardly wait to get to Quito and drive the Spaniards from that department. His chief commander for the campaign would be General Antonio José de Sucre, a young man Bolívar called "the bravest of the brave and the truest of the true."

At first, all went well. They were almost to the city of Popoyan when the Spanish commander came out to meet

90

them, surrendered, and asked if he and his forces might join Bolívar's army. Bolívar agreed and the Spaniards became loyal fighters for him.

Before long, though, the liberators had to climb the fierce Andes mountains again. Once more the rocky giants took their toll. Three thousand men began the climb. Two thousand finished it.

Their main battle against the Spanish took place on April 7, 1822, near Bombóna, still high in the mountains. From the start it looked as if Bolívar's army did not have a chance. Then one of his men, Valdez, actually led his men up the side of a cliff by having them stick their bayonets into crevices and use them as ladders. Their subsequent attack stunned and scattered the Spanish, who had run out of ammunition.

Many of the remaining battles for Quito were led by Sucre, who proved himself to be as brave and true as Bolívar had said he was. By the middle of 1822, Quito was a free department of the Republic of Colombia.

By that time, Bolívar was tired. He had been very ill with a fever in Quito and now that that job had been done, he wanted to go home to rest and spend some time with his family. He did not get the chance. Instead, while he was still in Guayaquil in Quito, he received a visitor.

José de San Martín was an Argentine general whom many people have called "the best soldier in South America." While Bolívar had been fighting for the freedom of the countries in the northern part of South America, San Martín had been doing the same thing in the south.

Thanks to him, Argentina and Chile were now free, but San Martín knew that no South American country would be safe while Spain still held Peru. He also knew that he could not free that country without Bolívar's help.

So the two men met privately to see what they could work out. It was a meeting doomed to failure. Given time, they could have agreed on how many men Bolívar would supply and who would command them. It was what would happen to Peru *after* the Spanish were gone that caused their problem.

San Martín was a monarchist. He believed that the hereditary rule of kings and queens was the best government a country could have. True, he did not want the Spanish ruling Peru. But after they were gone, he wanted to ask some other European royal family to take over. Bolívar was horrified. Such an idea went against everything he had been fighting for. He did not believe that South American people were ready for total democracy, but they certainly did not need kings and queens. On this point he would not yield and neither would San Martín.

So the proposed alliance failed and a grim-faced San Martín, at age forty-four, retired and moved to France. He could not win without Bolívar and he would not win with him. Retirement was all that was left for him.

The Peruvian rebels fought on, though, and Bolívar promptly sent two battalions to help them. The battalions returned. Peru's army did not want them. It would fight its own battles.

That proud attitude changed quickly at the beginning of 1823 when Spain handed the Peruvians two severe losses. Meekly the army asked Bolívar for help. He gave it at once, both in the form of troops and with one of his most trusted officers, General Sucre. In September, he went himself with an army to see how things were going.

They were in a terrible—and all too familiar—mess. The Peruvian officers could not get along with one another. The president, vice-president, and minister of war changed sides and joined up with the Spanish. The congress did not know what to do—except to give Bolívar full power over the government and the army. He took it, and then immediately became ill.

In spite of all this, by early August 1823, Bolívar had whipped together an army and stood ready to meet the Spaniards at Junin, another battlefield high in the mountains. This time it took his forces less than an hour to win.

The last great battle in Peru—and South America—took place in Ayacucho, 9,200 feet above sea level. Bolívar was not there. The Colombian congress had decided that he could not be president of Peru and lead a Colombian army.

But once again, General Sucre justified Bolívar's faith in

him. He led the forces brilliantly and soundly defeated a much larger Spanish army. One story says that when Bolívar heard the news of this victory, he ripped off his military tunic, threw it on the floor, and stamped on it. "Thank God!" he cried. "I will never have to command an army again."

Chapter 13

GLORY—AND DISAPPOINTMENT

Cheers. Letters of congratulation. Promises of statues. Money. The whole world honored Bolívar as a hero now and many people wanted to reward him. George Washington's descendants even sent him a gold medal that the first president of the United States had owned. They called him "the second Washington of the New World." Others had different names for him. "Emperor of the Andes" had a nice ring, said some. Páez firmly believed he should declare himself Simón I, king of Venezuela. But Bolívar had no desire to become either an emperor or a king.

In 1825, though, he was offered yet another office. Upper Peru—the southeastern part of that country—became a separate nation and chose him as its president for life. Bolívar declined. Instead, he told the assembly they should have Antonio José de Sucre, the young general—now a field marshal—who also had done much to win them their liberty. The new nation agreed, but did decide to call itself Bolívar. (Later that was changed to Bolivia.)

Of course Bolívar reveled in all the fuss. Too often in the past, his victories and accomplishments had been swallowed up by political squabbling. It felt very good to see them shine for a change. But he was not at all interested in the financial rewards offered him. Money had never mattered much to Bolívar. For years he had used his own resources to help pay his soldiers or to establish pensions for their families when they were killed in battle. When the Peruvian congress wanted to give him a million pesos, he suggested they use the money to help people in war-ravaged towns instead.

He did allow himself one special reward. A few years earlier, he had met and fallen in love with an unusual young woman called Manuela Sáenz. She was beautiful, strong, clever, brave, and full of life. She also was married to an Englishman. But as time passed, both she and Bolívar chose to ignore that inconvenient fact. Manuela loved to ride, fence, and shoot. Dressed in a man's uniform and riding a white stallion, she followed Bolívar into battle in Quito, much to the delight of the other soldiers. When they killed a Spaniard, they would cut off his mustache and give it to her. They called her "La Libertadora."

Bolívar felt he must leave Manuela behind during campaigns in Peru. But once the fighting was over, he wanted her company again and she was more than ready to come to him. Soon she became the darling of Lima. During the day she rode through the streets in a uniform she designed herself or played with the many animals she kept as pets, including a bear cub. At night she presided over the glittering social events Bolívar loved to hold at his villa. In her presence, Bolívar could relax and he needed relaxation badly.

At the same time, Bolívar had work to do. He wanted to travel through Peru and learn more about this country that insisted on calling him its dictator. He also wanted to improve living conditions, education, and the plight of the Indians. He saw some strange sights during that eight-month journey, including Lake Titicaca, over a hundred miles long, and Potosí, a city with a mountain made of silver.

He also received news of an old friend—Simón Rodríguez, his former teacher. Rodríguez's wanderings had somehow brought him to Bogotá, where Bolívar wrote to him and invited him to come to him. Before long, Rodríguez showed up, ragged and idealistic as ever.

Meanwhile, Bolívar had agreed to write a constitution for Bolivia, a task he always enjoyed. Once again he insisted that slavery must be abolished. He also asked for freedom of religion, but the final version adopted by the assembly declared the state religion to be Roman Catholicism.

Bolívar left Bolivia another gift that did not go over as well as the constitution. He made Simón Rodríguez head of the school system. It was not a good choice. Rodríguez had no idea of how to manage funds and his educational ideas shocked and angered the people. The last straw came when he began teaching his classes in the nude. Soon he was gone, wandering the world again.

About this time, Bolívar was hard at work trying to realize a dream that he had held dear for years—a congress or organization of South American nations that would meet in Panamá with other free countries to discuss matters important to all of them. He saw such a group as a vital force for peace and cooperation and had high hopes for its success.

Invited to the congress of Panamá were most of the Latin American governments as well as those of England and the United States. But when it met in 1826, only Mexico, Guatemala, Peru, Colombia, and England sent representatives. Furthermore, the English representative was allowed only to observe, not participate, and those from the other four nations had no real power to speak for their governments. All in all, the congress of Panamá was a dismal failure and a bitter disappointment to Bolívar. There was no way that he could know that many years later, first the Pan-American Union and then the Organization of American States would take root and flourish from the seeds he had planted.

The failure of his congress was only one of many troubles that began to swarm around Bolívar now. Peru kept bickering with her neighbors and war threatened to break out any day. The Republic of Colombia simply could not regard itself as one nation and looked as if it might break apart in the next strong political wind. As Bolívar had feared, Santander in Bogotá and Páez in Caracas were contributing to these problems. If he did not want to see everything he had worked for vanish into chaos, he had better get back to Colombia as quickly as possible.

A monument to Simón Bolívar in Cartagena

Chapter 14

PLOWING THE SEA

Bolívar arrived at Bogotá ill and exhausted. He saw at once that Santander had been up to his old tricks, trying to convince the people that Bolívar was their enemy while he, Santander, was their friend. It did not take Bolívar long to switch their loyalties back to him. He was still as inspiring—and charming—as he had ever been.

Eleven days after he arrived, he was ready to leave again. Now his destination was Venezuela where he hoped to straighten out the mess Páez had made. Mariño was not helping matters either, although Arismendi and Bermúdez remained loyal to Bolívar.

Once again the people themselves turned the tide in favor of their Liberator. Before he even got there, they were singing his praises and Páez wisely decided to join them. In a shrewd move of his own, Bolívar publicly announced that he forgave Páez and made his third and final triumphal entry into Caracas.

That triumph did not last long. He had barely settled into a happy reunion with his sisters, old Hipólita, and Matea when he received word of more trouble back in New Granada. Santander was using his forgiveness of Páez to make him look bad among the people. At the same time, Bolivia had decided to throw out his constitution.

In the period that followed, Bolívar must have felt as if he were trying to hold together a giant crumbling building with his bare hands. He rushed back to Bogotá and again won the people's support. Then he spent a few months trying to rest with Manuela at his country home not far from the city. At once Santander got busy spreading rumors and even writing newspaper articles that claimed Bolívar wanted to be king.

In February of 1828, Páez sent word that Spanish ships from Puerto Rico planned to attack Venezuela. Bolívar gathered his army and marched off. But before he reached the border, he learned that the ships had gone. Back to Bogotá, he thought. Then came word that a general had staged a revolt at Cartagena. So he headed in that direction. When he was halfway there, he found out that the revolt had been crushed.

The next big event would be a convention at Ocaña. Its job was to come up with a constitution for the Republic of Colombia. But Bolívar was simply too exhausted to attend. Instead he rested in the little village of Bucaramanga and read daily reports of the convention's progress. In the long run, it did nothing except state that the old constitution was no good.

A group of citizens begged Bolívar to come back to Bogotá

and put the government in order once more. He sighed and went. This time he and Manuela would live in the government palace. He had been appointed dictator for the next two years. But even that did not stop Santander and his men.

Late on September 25, 1828, Bolívar woke up to the sound of barking dogs. Then he heard shouts and gunfire. They came, he realized suddenly, from inside the palace itself. He and Manuela jumped out of bed. Bolívar grabbed his sword and headed for the door. By then he could hear the words the men were shouting.

"Death to Bolívar!"

Horrified, Manuela shoved him back. Did he think he could fight those men single-handed? He must escape through the window. It was not far to the ground. And she had a plan for getting rid of the men. A moment later, the heavy door caved in and the gang of assassins stared foolishly at a furious Manuela who waved a sword in their faces. They wanted Bolívar, did they? Well, he was not here. He was at the Council Hall. He had been there all night.

The men cursed and hurried away to search the rest of the palace. They killed several of Bolívar's men and wounded others. But they did not find him. By then, he and his head servant, José Palacio, were hiding under one of the city bridges. They stayed there until dawn when voices overhead informed them that Bolívar's men had overcome the mob.

Their leaders were arrested, tried, and found guilty—including Santander, who was sentenced to death. For reasons of his own, Bolívar changed that sentence to exile. It was as if he knew that Santander could never hurt him again.

But in spite of his escape and the defeat of his enemies, something inside Bolívar seemed to die that September night. Outside events continued to hurt and disappoint him, but nothing could surprise him anymore.

Bolovia and Peru were already fighting and Sucre had resigned as president back in August. In a period of only five days, Bolivia had three new presidents and murdered two of them. Early in 1829, Peru attacked Colombia.

Bolívar tried hard to hold his republic together by ruling more harshly. They had asked for a dictator. Now they would have one. But he was too tired and too ill to continue in this way for very long. On January 20, 1830, he resigned his dictatorship in Bogotá.

"My one desire," he told the congress, "has been to contribute to your liberty."

Then he went back to his country home to rest. When he felt better, he would leave Colombia for good. Maybe he would go to France or England. He was not sure yet. What he did feel sure about was that his life's work had been in vain. By now Venezuela had seceded from the republic. Soon Quito would do the same. He was no longer welcome in

Venezuela and before long Colombia would want to be rid of him too.

At the moment, however, he had no money for travel. His niece must sell the mines—all he owned now in Venezuela—and send him the proceeds. Meanwhile, he would head for the coast.

On May 8, 1830, Bolívar rode away from Bogotá for the last time, leaving Manuela behind. Perhaps, he said, he could send for her later when he had found a new home. A British officer watched him leave. "He is gone," said the officer, "the great gentleman of Colombia."

Down the Magdalena River Bolívar traveled, each batch of news bringing him fresh insults from old friends—Páez, Bermúdez, Arismendi. They were calling him "tyrant" now and "a creature of evil purposes." He found a little cabin outside Cartagena and settled in to wait for the money from his mines. Instead, he received the cruelest news of all. Sucre had been murdered. He had been riding from Bogotá to Quito when he was ambushed.

Soon afterward, Bolívar received messages from Bogotá, Caracas, and Cartagena itself. People in all three places wanted him to return and rule them. Their pleas came too late. Bolívar was dying and he knew it.

"Those who fight in South America's revolution," he said to a friend, "plow the sea."

Heat and rain drove him from Cartagena down the coast

to Barranquilla. But conditions there were no better, so he decided to sail to Jamaica. He had only been aboard the ship a little while, though, when he became violently ill. So they took him back to Santa Marta and in that village he lay and waited for death. Two different doctors had diagnosed tuberculosis. They could give him medicines, but they held out no hope for his recovery.

In these last days, Bolívar turned again to his favorite book from childhood, *Don Quixote*. People had called that idealistic knight a fool and a madman. Well, they could say the same thing now about him.

On December 7, friends carried him to a house outside the village. Ironically, it belonged to a Spanish officer, Joaquín de Mier. One of Bolívar's lifelong enemies would give him his last home on earth. By this time, he was often delirious with fever. One of the people who had stayed with him was José Palacio, the servant with whom he had hid under the bridge. Sometimes in his confusion, he cried out to Palacio.

"José, bring the luggage. They do not want us here!"

On December 17, 1830, at one o'clock in the afternoon, Simón Bolívar died. He was forty-seven years old.

Chapter 15

LATER

Manuela Sáenz worked for Bolívar's cause in Bogotá until she received word that he was dying. Then she hurried to be with him. She was not in time.

The years that followed took her to a dungeon in Cartagena, to exile in Jamaica, back to her homeland of Ecuador, and finally to the coastal town of Paita in Peru. There, with the little money she had left, she rented a rickety building and opened a tobacco shop.

Day after day, she sat in the doorway, crocheting and selling cigars to the whalers whose ships put in at Paita. From all accounts, she was still a beautiful and gracious woman, but much quieter and more peaceful than she had been in the past.

When she was almost fifty, a rotted board gave way beneath her foot and she fell down an entire flight of stairs. From then on, she was bedridden with a dislocated hip. No longer able to run her shop, she had to depend on gifts from the townspeople to keep her alive.

Sometimes, though, she still had visitors—old friends who were not afraid to associate with her, or strangers curious to meet the woman who had captured the Liberator's heart.

One day a shabby old man stumbled in. It was Simón Rodríguez, eighty now, and finally finished wandering. He found a hut not far from Manuela where he wrote letters for people to earn money for food and visited her whenever he could. In 1854, he died. His last words were, "The comedy is finished."

In November of 1856, a sailor brought diphtheria to Paita. Scores of people died, including, on November 23, Manuela Sáenz. She was fifty-eight years old. Because of the epidemic, the town buried her in a common grave with other victims and burned all of her possessions.

Legend says that another woman also hurried to be with Bolívar as he lay dying. Anita Lenoit traveled from Tenerife to Cartagena, then walked sixty miles through jungle to Barranquilla.

Illness kept her there for a while, but at last she found a boat to take her to Santa Marta. She arrived one day too late. Her seventeen years of waiting ended as she followed the body of the man she loved to the cemetery.

Bolívar died almost penniless and was buried in a borrowed nightshirt. During the period that followed his death, his political enemies branded him with every vile name they could think of and decreed that he be forgotten in the annals of South American history.

But twelve years after his death, the tide turned. His sisters had begun the process, begging for the return of his body to Caracas. Soon others took up the cause.

Late in 1842, an international fleet of vessels stood guard in the harbor of Santa Marta. Among their flags, flying at half-mast, were those of the countries Bolívar had liberated. His body was carried in state to a barge and taken out to a man-of-war. The entire fleet escorted it to La Guaira.

On December 17, a great funeral procession wound through the streets of Caracas, under specially built arches, past draped buildings and silent crowds. Two old black women watched it, their eyes dim with tears. At the end, it was Hipólita and Matea who paid last honors to the child they had nursed and saw him safely home.

Simón Bolívar 1783-1830

1783 Bolívar is born in Caracas, Venezuela, on July 24. Great Britain recognizes the independence of the U.S. A paddle-wheel boat is sailed on the Saône River in France.

1784 Swiss inventor Aimé Argand designs the oil burner. The first balloon ascends in England. The first school for the blind is established in England.

1785 A seismograph is invented for measuring earthquakes. James Watt and Matthew Boulton install a steam engine with rotary motion in a cotton-spinning factory in England. Jean-Pierre-François Blanchard and John Jeffries cross the English Channel in a balloon.

1786 American inventor James Rumsey designs the first mechanically driven boat. Early attempts at internal gas lighting are made in Germany and England. A golf club is founded in Charleston, South Carolina.

1787 The constitution of the U.S. is signed. The federal U.S. government is established. John Fitch launches a steamboat on the Delaware River. Dollar currency is introduced in the U.S.

1788 New York is declared federal capital of the U.S. The first cigar factory is opened in Germany.

1789 The first U.S. Congress opens in New York. George Washington is inaugurated president of the U.S. In Paris, a mob storms the Bastille, beginning the French Revolution. The first steam-driven cotton factory is established in Manchester, England.

1790 Philadelphia becomes the federal capital of the U.S. Washington, D.C. is founded.

1791 The first ten amendments to the U.S. constitution (Bill of Rights) are ratified. The waltz becomes fashionable in England. William Wilberforce's motion for abolition of the slave trade in England is carried through Parliament.

1792 French Revolution ends; France becomes a republic. Denmark is the first nation to abolish the slave trade. Two political parties are formed in the U.S.: the Republican under Thomas Jefferson and the Federalist under Alexander Hamilton and John Adams.

1793 The Louvre in Paris becomes a national art gallery. The building of the Capitol is begun in Washington, D.C. Sir Alexander Mackenzie is the first to cross Canada from coast to coast. Eli Whitney invents the cotton gin. U.S. law compels escaped slaves to return to their owners.

1794 The U.S. navy is established. Slavery is abolished in French colonies.

1795 The Treaty of Lorenzo between U.S. and Spain settles the boundary with Florida and gives the U.S. the right to navigate the Mississippi River. The metric system is adopted in France. The first horse-drawn railroad is built in England.

1796 George Washington, refusing to serve a third term, delivers his Farewell Address. Napoleon Bonaparte marries Josephine de Beauharnais. English physician Edward Jenner introduces a vaccination against smallpox.

1797 Napoleon, appointed to command forces for the invasion of England, arrives in Paris. John Adams is inaugurated president of the U.S. England begins to export iron. The first copper pennies are minted in England.

1798 The Battle of the Pyramids makes Napoleon master of Egypt. An income tax is introduced in England as a wartime measure.

1799 Bolívar goes to Spain. The Rosetta Stone (now at the British Museum in London) is found near Rosetta, Egypt, and makes the deciphering of hieroglyphics possible.

1800 Napoleon's army defeats Austrians and conquers Italy. U.S. capital is moved to Washington, D.C. Thomas Jefferson wins U.S. presidential election. Eli Whitney makes muskets with interchangeable parts. Letter post is introduced in Berlin, Germany.

1801 Bolívar goes to Paris, France. Act of Union of Great Britain and Ireland comes into force.

American civil engineer Robert Fulton produces the first submarine—*Nautilus*. The Union Jack becomes the official flag of Great Britain and Ireland.

1802 Bolívar marries María Teresa in Madrid; they return to Venezuela. Alexander von Humboldt almost succeeds in climbing Mount Chimborao in Ecuador. Napoleon becomes president of the Italian Republic. John Dalton introduces atomic theory into chemistry. The term "biology" is coined in Germany.

1803 María Teresa dies in Venezuela on January 22. At the end of the year Bolívar goes to Spain. U.S. buys large tract of land from Gulf of Mexico to northwest, including Louisiana and New Orleans, from France (Louisiana Purchase). Swiss cantons regain independence. Robert Fulton propels a boat by steam power.

1804 Bolívar and other Creoles are forced to leave Spain; Bolívar goes to Paris. Napoleon proclaims himself emperor of the French. Alexander Hamilton, former U.S. secretary of the treasury, is killed in a duel with Aaron Burr. The first dahlias are grown in England.

1807 Bolívar returns to Caracas. U.S. passes an Embargo Act against Britain and France. France invades Portugal; dethroned royal family flees to Brazil. Robert Fulton's steamboat *Clermont* navigates on the Hudson River. England prohibits slave trade. London, England, streets are lit by gas.

1808 Napoleon sets up his brother Joseph as king of Spain. U.S. prohibits importation of slaves from Africa. Pigtails for men's hair disappear from fashion. Extensive excavations are begun for the lost city of Pompeii, Italy.

1809 The French army takes Vienna. Napoleon annexes the Papal States. Napoleon divorces Josephine. Ecuador gains independence from Spain.

1810 Spain sends new governor, Vicente de Emparán, to Venezuela. Bolívar fights under General Francisco de Miranda in revolt against Spanish in Venezuela. Bolívar appoints a diplomat to England and emerges as a major figure in South American politics. Techniques for canning food are developed.

1811 Venezuela declares its independence. Paraguay also breaks away from Spain. Johann Meyer, a Swiss mountaineer, climbs the Jungfrau.

1812 Bolívar plans Venezuelan revolution. Earthquake hits Caracas and other Venezuelan towns. U.S. declares war on Britain. James Madison is elected U.S. president. A machine is invented for spinning flax.

1813 Bolívar travels to Curacao and then to New Granada (Colombia). Bolívar writes for the Granadan newspapers and his writings become known as the Manifesto of Cartagena. Caracas city council appoints Bolívar captain-general of the army. Mexico declares her independence. The waltz conquers European ballrooms.

1814 Bolívar is finally defeated in Venezuela and leaves for Colombia; captures Bogotá, but is defeated. Napoleon abdicates and is banished to Elba. British force burns Washington, D.C. The London *Times* is printed by steam-operated press. Westminster, London, is the first district to be illuminated by gas.

1815 Bolívar flees to Jamaica; composes Jamaica Letter. First Duke of Wellington, Arthur Wellesley, and Gebhard Leberecht von Blücher defeat Napoleon at Waterloo. Napoleon is banished to St. Helena. Brazil declares herself an independent empire. The miner's safety lamp is invented.

1816 Bolívar flees to Haiti and plans another successful revolution in Venezuela. Argentina is declared independent. James Monroe is elected president of the U.S. The kaleidoscope is invented. The stethoscope is invented. Economic crisis in England causes large-scale emigration to Canada and the U.S.

1817 Bolívar establishes the independent government of Venezuela. U.S. begins construction of the Erie Canal.

1818 The border between Canada and the U.S. (the 49th parallel) is agreed upon. The *Savannah* becomes the first steamship to cross the Atlantic. Professional horse racing begins in the U.S.

1819 Bolívar enters New Granada; leads army over Andes to liberate Bogotá. Bolívar is made president of Republic of Colombia and is given supreme power. Bolívar publishes "Fundamental Laws of the Republic of Colombia."

1820 Revolution in Spain; King Ferdinand VII is forced to restore Constitution of 1812. In the U.S., the Missouri Compromise: Maine enters Union as free state, Missouri, as slave state. The Washington Colonization Society founds Liberia for the repatriation of Negroes.

1821 Bolívar wins Battle of Carabobo, the final victory for independence of Venezuela. Bolívar marches south to Quito and Peru. Peru proclaimed independent from Spain, followed by Guatemala, Panama, and Santo Domingo. Sound reproduction is demonstrated by Sir Charles Wheatstone.

1822 Bolívar battles the Spanish near Bombóna. Quito becomes a free department of the Republic of Colombia. Brazil becomes independent of Portugal. Greeks adopt liberal republican constitution and proclaim independence. Louis-Jacques-Mande Daguerre and Charles-Marie Bouton invent the diorama, paintings illuminated in a dark room to give an illusion of reality. Lenses for lighthouses are invented.

1823 Bolívar defeats the Spanish at the Battle of Junin. Mexico becomes a republic. Guatemala, San Salvador, Nicaragua, Honduras, and Costa Rica form the Confederation of United Provinces of Central America. The Monroe Doctrine closes the American continent to colonial settlements by foreign powers. Charles Macintosh invents waterproof fabric. Rugby football originates at Rugby School, England.

1824 Peru is freed from Spain. Bolívar is proclaimed emperor of Peru. John Quincy Adams is elected president of the U.S. The Erie Canal is finished.

1825 Bolívar visits upper Peru, organizing new republic, called Bolivia. Portugal recognizes Brazilian independence. Horse-drawn buses begin operating in London, England. Tea roses from China are introduced in Europe.

1826 The Royal Zoological Society is founded in London, England. The first railroad tunnel opens on the Liverpool-Manchester line in England.

1827 Peru secedes from Colombia. Joseph Niepce produces photographs on a metal plate. George Ohm formulates Ohm's Law, defining electrical current potential and resistance. James Simpson constructs sand filter for purification of London's water supply. Sulfur friction matches are introduced by John Walker.

1828 Bolívar returns to Botogá. Uruguay (since 1821 part of Brazil) becomes independent republic following Treaty of Rio de Janeiro. Andrew Jackson is elected president of the U.S. Charles Carroll of Carrollton, the richest American of his time, inaugurates construction of the Baltimore & Ohio Railroad, the first railroad built in the U.S. for the transportation of passengers and freight. Karl Baedeker publishes his guidebook, *The Rhine from Mainz to Cologne.*

1829 Slavery is abolished in Mexico. There is instability in Bolivia, Peru, and Colombia. Physicist John Henry constructs an early version of the electromagnetic motor. James Smithson bequeaths 100,000 pounds to found the Smithsonian Institution in the United States. The first U.S. patent on a typewriter is granted to William Burt of Detroit. The first Oxford-Cambridge Boat Race takes place at Henley, England.

1830 Bolívar resigns dictatorship in Colombia and dies near Santa Marta, Gran Colombia. Ecuador secedes from Gran Colombia and becomes an independent republic. Belva Lockwood, an American lawyer, is the first woman to practice before the Supreme Court and be nominated for the presidency.

INDEX- *Page numbers in boldface type indicate illustrations.*

ABOUT THE AUTHOR

Carol Greene has degrees in English literature and musicology. She has worked in international exchange programs, as an editor, and as a teacher. She now lives in St. Louis, Missouri, and writes full time. She has published over seventy books, most of them for children. Other Childrens Press biographies by Ms. Greene include *Louisa May Alcott, Marie Curie, Thomas Alva Edison, Hans Christian Andersen, Marco Polo,* and *Wolfgang Amadeus Mozart* in the People of Distinction series; *Sandra Day O'Connor, Mother Teresa, Indira Nehru Gandhi, Diana, Princess of Wales, Desmond Tutu,* and *Elie Wiesel* in the Picture-Story Biography series; and *Benjamin Franklin* and *Pocahontas* in the Rookie Biographies.